W9-ANU-240

DATE DUE		

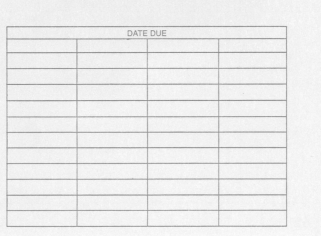

WEEKLY **WR** READER®
EARLY LEARNING LIBRARY

My Day at School/
Mi día en la escuela

In the Classroom/
En el salón de clases

by/por Joanne Mattern

Reading consultant/Consultora de lectura:
Susan Nations, M.Ed.,
author, literacy coach,
consultant in literacy development/
autora, tutora de alfabetización,
consultora de desarrollo de la lectura

Please visit our web site at: www.garethstevens.com
For a free color catalog describing Weekly Reader® Early Learning Library's list
of high-quality books, call 1-877-445-5824 (USA) or 1-800-387-3178 (Canada).
Weekly Reader® Early Learning Library's fax: (414) 336-0164.

Library of Congress Cataloging-in-Publication Data

Mattern, Joanne, 1963-
    In the classroom = En el salón de clases / by/por Joanne Mattern.
      p. cm. — (My day at school = Mi día en la escuela)
    Includes bibliographical references and index.
    ISBN-10: 0-8368-7361-0 — ISBN-13: 978-0-8368-7361-0 (lib. bdg.)
    ISBN-10: 0-8368-7368-8 — ISBN-13: 978-0-8368-7368-9 (softcover)
    1. Classroom environment—Juvenile literature.   2. School children—Juvenile literature.
   I. Title. II. Title: En el salón de clases.
   LC210.M38   2006
   372.18—dc22   2006018022

This edition first published in 2007 by
Weekly Reader® Early Learning Library
A Member of the WRC Media Family of Companies
330 West Olive Street, Suite 100
Milwaukee, WI 53212 USA

Editor: Barbara Kiely Miller
Art direction: Tammy West
Cover design and page layout: Kami Strunsee
Picture research: Diane Laska-Swanke
Photographs: © John Sibilski Photography
Translators: Tatiana Acosta and Guillermo Gutiérrez

Printed in the United States of America

1 2 3 4 5 6 7 8 9 10 09 08 07 06

Note to Educators and Parents

Reading is such an exciting adventure for young children! They are beginning to integrate their oral language skills with written language. To encourage children along the path to early literacy, books must be colorful, engaging, and interesting; they should invite the young reader to explore both the print and the pictures.

The *My Day at School* series is designed to help young readers review the routines and rules of a school day, while learning new vocabulary and strengthening their reading comprehension. In simple, easy-to-read language, each book follows a child through part of a typical school day.

Each book is specially designed to support the young reader in the reading process. The familiar topics are appealing to young children and invite them to read — and re-read — again and again. The full-color photographs and enhanced text further support the student during the reading process.

In addition to serving as wonderful picture books in schools, libraries, homes, and other places where children learn to love reading, these books are specifically intended to be read within an instructional guided reading group. This small group setting allows beginning readers to work with a fluent adult model as they make meaning from the text. After children develop fluency with the text and content, the book can be read independently. Children and adults alike will find these books supportive, engaging, and fun!

— Susan Nations, M.Ed., author, literacy coach,
and consultant in literacy development

Nota para los maestros y los padres

¡Leer es una aventura tan emocionante para los niños pequeños! A esta edad están comenzando a integrar su manejo del lenguaje oral con el lenguaje escrito. Para animar a los niños en el camino de la lectura incipiente, los libros deben ser coloridos, estimulantes e interesantes; deben invitar a los jóvenes lectores a explorar la letra impresa y las ilustraciones.

La serie *Mi día en la escuela* está pensada para ayudar a los jóvenes lectores a repasar las actividades y normas de un día de escuela, mientras enriquecen su vocabulario y refuerzan su comprensión. Cada libro presenta, en un lenguaje sencillo y fácil de entender, las actividades de un niño durante parte de un típico día escolar.

Cada libro está especialmente diseñado para ayudar al joven lector en el proceso de lectura. Los temas familiares llaman la atención de los niños y los invitan a leer —y releer— una y otra vez. Las fotografías a todo color y el tamaño de la letra ayudan aún más al estudiante en el proceso de lectura.

Además de servir como maravillosos libros ilustrados en escuelas, bibliotecas, hogares y otros lugares donde los niños aprenden a amar la lectura, estos libros han sido especialmente concebidos para ser leídos en un grupo de lectura guiada. Este contexto permite que los lectores incipientes trabajen con un adulto que domina la lectura mientras van determinando el significado del texto. Una vez que los niños dominan el texto y el contenido, el libro puede ser leído de manera independiente. ¡Estos libros les resultarán útiles, estimulantes y divertidos a niños y a adultos por igual!

— Susan Nations, M.Ed., autora/tutora de alfabetización/
consultora de desarrollo de la lectura

This is my **classroom** at school.

I have lots of fun here.

— — — — — — — — — — — —

Éste es mi **salón de clases** en la escuela. Aquí me divierto mucho.

We sit in our chairs. Our teacher calls our names. We are all here today.

Nos sentamos en nuestras sillas. La maestra dice nuestros nombres. Hoy hemos venido todos.

We take turns reading. Our
teacher helps us with hard words.

— — — — — — — — — — — — —

Nos turnamos para leer.
La maestra nos ayuda con
las palabras difíciles.

Then we write our own stories.

I print my story neatly.

— — — — — — — — — — — — — — — —

Después escribimos nuestros

propios cuentos. Yo escribo

mi cuento con cuidado.

Now it is time for **math**. We are learning to add numbers. I know the answer.

Es la hora de las **matemáticas**.

Estamos aprendiendo a sumar.

Yo sé la respuesta.

Then it is time for **science**. We are learning how plants grow.

- - - - - - - - - - - - -

Después es la hora de estudiar **ciencias**. Estamos aprendiendo cómo crecen las plantas.

We do different things after lunch. Some days we have art. Today we have music.

‒ ‒ ‒ ‒ ‒ ‒ ‒ ‒ ‒ ‒ ‒ ‒ ‒ ‒

Después del almuerzo hacemos diferentes cosas. Algunos días tenemos clases de arte. Hoy tenemos música.

We go to the **library**. My teacher helps me find a good book.

- - - - - - - - - - - -

Vamos a la **biblioteca**. Mi maestra me ayuda a encontrar un buen libro.

It is time to go home. I pack
my books. See you tomorrow!

— — — — — — — — — — — — —

Es hora de ir a casa. Recojo
mis libros. ¡Hasta mañana!

Glossary

classroom — a room in a school where classes take place

library — a place that has many books for people to borrow and read

math — short for "mathematics," which is the study of numbers, shapes, and measurements

science — the study of nature and living things

Glosario

biblioteca — lugar donde se guardan libros para leer o sacar prestados

ciencias — el estudio de la naturaleza

matemáticas — el estudio de los números, las figuras y las medidas

salón de clases — cuarto de una escuela donde se dan las clases

For More Information/Más información

Books

The Library. I Like to Visit (series).
  Jacqueline Laks Gorman (Gareth Stevens)

Lunch Money and Other Poems About School.
  Carol Shields (Puffin)

Teacher. People in My Community (series).
  JoAnn Early Macken (Gareth Stevens)

Libros

The Library/La biblioteca. I Like to Visit/Me gusta visitar (series).
  Jacqueline Laks Gorman (Gareth Stevens)

Teacher/El maestro. People in My Community/La gente de
  mi comunidad (series). JoAnn Early Macken (Gareth Stevens)

Index

art 16
books 18, 20
classrooms 4
libraries 18
math 12
music 16
numbers 12
plants 14
reading 8

science 14
stories 10
teachers 6, 8, 18
words 8
writing 10

Índice

arte 16
bibliotecas 18
ciencias 14
cuentos 10
escribir 10
leer 8
libros 18, 20
maestros 6, 8, 18

matemáticas 12
música 16
números 12
palabras 8
plantas 14
salón de clases 4

About the Author

Joanne Mattern has written more than one hundred and fifty books for children. Joanne also works in her local library. She lives in New York State with her husband, three daughters, and assorted pets. She enjoys animals, music, going to baseball games, reading, and visiting schools to talk about her books.

Información sobre la autora

Joanne Mattern ha escrito más de ciento cincuenta libros para niños. Además, Joanne trabaja en la biblioteca de su comunidad. Vive en el estado de Nueva York con su esposo, sus tres hijas y varias mascotas. A Joanne le gustan los animales, la música, ir al béisbol, leer y hacer visitas a las escuelas para hablar de sus libros.